War of the Woods

WOODS

The Pacific Northwest Logging Argument

by Terry Miller Shannon

ZB **Zaner-Bloser**
The Language Arts and Reading Company

Table of Contents

Introduction

People argue about logging in the Pacific Northwest. The problem is that two groups of people have different purposes. One group is made up of loggers and **lumber** companies. This group wants to **harvest** the trees in the forest. They want to continue cutting trees down. They sell the trees as wood and wood products, such as boards, furniture, and paper.

The other group of people is called **environmentalists**. They believe logging hurts Earth. They fear cutting trees down will harm nature.

Forests of huge evergreen trees cover the Pacific Northwest. An evergreen tree does not shed its leaves in the winter. Evergreens often have needles instead of leaves. They often bear cones, such as pinecones. Firs, pines, and cedars are types of evergreen trees.

Evergreen forests blanket around eighty percent of western Oregon and Washington. There are many different kinds of evergreen trees in the area. Some Pacific Northwest evergreen trees are the biggest in the world.

The area has wet winters, dry summers, rich soil, and mild weather. Evergreen trees grow well in these conditions.

The trees are the area's natural wealth. Because of them, many people have had logging jobs for ages. People lose their jobs when logging is stopped or cut back.

Should the forests be cut? Many people are working to find an answer. People who are interested belong to different groups with different concerns. These people include government officials. People who like to spend time outdoors, such as hikers and campers, are also interested. Environmentalists are concerned about logging, too. Lumber companies and loggers also hope for an answer to the logging question.

Should we log the forests or not? This book will look into the subject of logging in the Northwest. This book discusses possible answers to the problem. Is there a way everyone can win?

CHAPTER I

Giving a Hoot About an Owl

You might see bumper stickers about logging. Some bumper stickers talk about the spotted owl. These are also about logging. One bumper sticker says, "Spotted owl tastes like chicken." The person with that bumper sticker wants the forests logged. Are you wondering what a bird has to do with turning trees into lumber?

Northern spotted owl

The northern spotted owl represents the logging argument. The owl lives in the area from northwestern California to British Columbia. The owl must live in "old growth forest." Old growth trees have never been logged. The trees are very old.

Old growth forest trees may be as young as 180 years old. Some are 1,000 years old! The older trees began growing around the time Leif Erickson discovered North America. His discovery was around 1000 A.D. That was over 400 years before Christopher Columbus set sail.

Just think. We can touch a living tree that grew centuries before the **Mayflower** arrived in the New World. Many people find this amazing. They feel the old growth trees are precious. It would take hundreds of years to replace a tree that old. Once it is gone, it is just a memory.

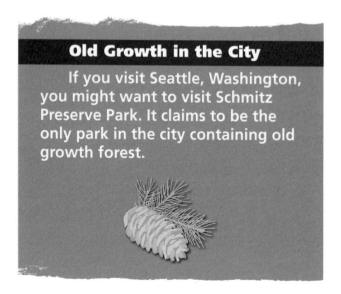

Old Growth in the City

If you visit Seattle, Washington, you might want to visit Schmitz Preserve Park. It claims to be the only park in the city containing old growth forest.

Counting the rings will tell how old this tree was.

Are you wondering how scientists can tell how old a tree is? They count the rings of a fallen or cut trunk. One ring equals one year. Scientists call this "age dating" a tree.

What types of trees are in an old growth forest? In Washington and Oregon, you might see spruce, fir, pine, hemlock, cedar, redwood, madrone, and tanoak trees.

An old growth forest has large live trees, large standing dead trees, and large logs from fallen trees. Dead trees are sometimes called snags. The forest also has trees of many different ages.

Spotted owl with a mouse

The old growth forest is home to many animals. Some of these animals are food for spotted owls. The owls eat flying squirrels, deer mice, wood rats, and other small animals. If an owl cannot eat these animals, it will not have baby owls. Logging shrinks the old growth forest the spotted owl needs to survive.

The spotted owls are endangered. This means they are in danger of dying out. In order to save them, the old growth forests must not be logged.

Why does the spotted owl have such a hard life? A spotted owl has two babies every other year. Many young owls die before they are one year old. Larger birds, illness, and starvation kill the owls. Owls also die when logging ruins a nest. To live and have baby owls, a pair of adult owls needs lots of space. They need between 2,000 and 4,200 acres of old growth forest.

Young owls must find their own areas after they leave the nest. They will die if they cannot find their areas. If the young owls must travel far to find their areas, other animals often kill them. Traveling far is dangerous. Large areas of old growth forest are necessary, or spotted owls won't last.

Lumber companies want to cut down the old growth forests. They make a lot of money from each big, old tree. The government said the spotted owl was endangered during the 1990s. They stopped logging in many forests to save the owl. Many people working in lumber companies were out of work.

Environmentalists believe the spotted owl represents healthy forests. They believe if the owl is in danger, the forests are, too. They want to save the old growth forests full of **ancient** trees. They also want to save natural areas that might be ruined by logging.

When environmentalists protest logging, they may do it in many ways. The protesters lead marches to protest logging.

Some protesters have sat in trees for days or weeks to keep the trees from being cut down. Others have chained themselves to road gates so logging trucks can't pass through. Some environmentalists have damaged logging equipment. Environmentalists have **sued** lumber companies and the government to stop logging.

Loggers are angry about their lost jobs. They wonder how owls could be more important than their jobs.

Logging old growth forests **supported** many communities in Oregon, Washington, and northern California. These communities grew around mills that handled old growth and other lumber.

Loggers hate the forests being closed to save owls. They know the closing of the forest costs people lumber and jobs. Lumber companies know the trees in the areas closed to logging are worth a great deal of money.

Loggers and lumber companies want to cut and sell the valuable lumber. They also point out that logging is just one way forests are destroyed. When people clear land for building, making **pastures,** and planting gardens, forests are destroyed. **Mining** destroys forests, too.

As you can see, there are strong feelings on each side. Logging is not a simple subject. There are no easy answers to the question "Jobs or owls?"

Why Forests Matter

Forests are beautiful and peaceful. They are places to hike, fish, and camp. Forests provide homes for animals. Forests give us clean drinking water and homes for fish. The trees give us wood and paper goods we use every day. The trees improve and clean the air we breathe.

CHAPTER 2

History of Logging in the Pacific Northwest

How did lumber become so important? The history of logging will help us understand the strong feelings about it.

Pioneers traveled to the area in the nineteenth century. They needed land to build homes. They needed land to raise animals and grow crops. They burned the old growth forests to clear the land.

These men are in the remains of a burned forest.

There were once around 70 million acres of old growth forest in the area. People thought they could take wood from the forests forever. They believed the trees would never run out.

Lumber companies built mill towns in the 1800s. These towns had mills and homes for workers. Mill towns appeared first in Puget Sound, in the state of Washington. Later, mill towns dotted Oregon and Washington. Lumber traveled by boat at first. After 1900, trains carried lumber east.

The area's first mill was built in 1827. It was near Fort Vancouver, Washington. Soon, there were mills in the Oregon cities of Portland and Oregon City. The mills were sawmills that slice logs into boards.

The need for lumber grew and grew. Miners needed lumber to build towns during California's Gold Rush. Fires roared through Chicago, San Francisco, and other places. Lumber was needed to rebuild homes.

The rough land and big trees made logging hard. It was not easy to reach the trees. It was hard to take the trees to the mill. Loggers invented new ways to carry the logs. **Oxen** pulled logs across greased roads. Loggers sometimes floated logs in big ditches filled with water or through rivers. They built special train tracks to reach more trees.

Oxen pulled logs out of the forest.

This train is taking trees out of the forest.

New tools made logging easier. Loggers chopped trees down with axes until the late 1800s. Then, they discovered two-man saws. These saws cut trees easier and faster. Then, engineers invented steam engines to move logs to railroads or rivers. Loggers began climbing trees with safety belts and spiked boots in the early 1900s. Sawmills worked better and faster because of new tools.

These new tools cost a lot of money. Small companies couldn't afford them. They went out of business. Large companies could buy the new tools.

Some of the large companies came from the east coast of the United States. There wasn't much lumber left in the East. The companies moved west. Frederick Weyerhaeuser owned one company. He had made a fortune in lumber in the East.

Weyerhaeuser bought 900,000 acres of Northwest forest. He paid six dollars an acre. Other businessmen hurried to buy Pacific Northwest forests, too. They built hundreds of mills. The mills were busy because of the great need for wood. San Francisco was one city needing wood. People there wanted to rebuild their city after the 1906 earthquake.

Logging was one of the main businesses well into the twentieth century. There were lots of jobs and money after the world wars ended. People wanted lumber to build homes and businesses. The lumber business kept growing as cities grew.

Tools kept getting better. Loggers now used logging trucks, tractors, and chain saws. These tools made it faster and easier to log.

Loggers working in a forest do different jobs. One logger may be cutting a tree. Another may be wrapping wire around a log. Still another logger could be hauling logs. Yet another could be cutting logs. Another might be loading logs onto the logging truck.

The logs cut from forests are used in many ways other than just for buildings. Some become wood products, such as fences, floors, shipping boxes, firewood, and baseball bats. Other logs may be turned into paper for books, milk cartons, newspapers, magazines, cardboard, and tissue paper. Companies sometimes mix tiny wood pieces with chemicals to make carpet, fake leather, and fabric. The bark of the logs might be used in gardening or in making cork.

Washington was the biggest lumber state from 1905 to 1938. Sixty-three out of every hundred workers in Washington in 1910 worked in the lumber business. Oregon surpassed Washington to become the number one lumber state in 1938. Lumber supported many Pacific Northwest towns. Logging in **national** forests grew each year from 1945 to 1970.

Loggers kept cutting down trees. The old growth forests in the areas shrank.

Old growth forests covered around 15 million acres in the 1800s. They covered 5 million acres in 1985. The national government owns 4.8 million of those acres. The government allowed some logging in national forests.

Lumber companies logged most of the old growth forests owned by private individuals.

Forest fires raged in Oregon in 1987. The fires burned around 245,000 acres of forest. The destroyed wood's value was around 97.3 million dollars.

This firefighter is spraying water on a tree to keep a fire from spreading.

In 1989, the government listed the spotted owl as a **threatened** species. Courts insisted the government set aside old growth areas for the spotted owl in 1991.

Suddenly, there was much less logging on national land. Many people lost their jobs. Pacific Northwest mills began to close down.

However, lumber companies continued to cut wood on **private** land. Much of this wood was shipped overseas to Korea, Japan, and Taiwan.

Logs waiting to be shipped to Japan

The northern spotted owl represents the logging argument. Other animals also depend on old growth forests. Marbled murrelets and bald eagles are birds in danger of dying out. They need old growth forests in which to nest.

Other birds are not yet on the endangered list. But many people believe these birds are also in danger from logging:

- Northern goshawks
- Harlequin ducks
- Black-backed woodpeckers
- Pileated woodpeckers
- Vaux's swifts

Bald eagle

A rainbow trout swimming with red sockeye salmon

Fish are also at risk from logging. Dust and dirt settle into streams and rivers. Loggers cut trees that shaded and cooled streams. More sunshine reaches them. The water gets warmer. It can grow warm enough to kill **salmon** eggs. Some kinds of salmon and **trout** could disappear forever. Other water animals, such as **salamanders** and frogs, are also put in danger by logging.

CHAPTER 3

Concern Over Logging Methods

Some people worry about the ways wood is harvested from the forest. A forester is one person who can help decide the best way to care for a forest. She or he is someone who knows how to manage the forest. A forester wants to use the forest to help people.

The forester also wants to protect the forest's water, **wildlife,** and plants. Some foresters teach adults and children about the forests. Other foresters help with logging plans. Many work to regrow forests.

A forester may work with a person who owns a forest. One part of a forester's job is to know all the laws about forests.

One type of logging is called clear-cutting. Clear-cutting chops down every tree in an area. This is the cheapest way to log. It leaves one area of the forest completely bare.

Some people believe clear-cutting can be healthy for the forest because it is like a forest fire. Forest fires may be nature's way of clearing out areas. Forest fires do not strip the land completely. Some trees even thrive after a forest fire. Forest fires can help the soil.

Other people claim that poorly planned clear-cutting causes many problems. It destroys animals' homes. Clear-cutting may get rid of many animals living in the forest.

Clear-cutting also causes problems with water runoff. Without the trees, water flow is not slowed by tree roots. This can cause floods. Water sometimes wears away or erodes the land. It can wash dirt into streams and rivers. We know fish die when rivers, streams, and lakes become dirty. Snow gathers deeper in clear-cut areas. That snow will probably melt quickly. This leads to more problems with water and floods.

Aerial view of private land clear-cut up to the border of Gifford National Forest in Oregon

Thoughtful clear-cutting can cause less damage. Well-planned clear-cutting leaves small areas for wildlife. Care can be taken to use lighter equipment. Logging done on frozen ground upsets the soil less. It is better for allowing plants to grow again.

Another kind of logging is **selective** logging. Loggers cut just a few trees. They leave most of the forest alone. Many people think selective logging is a better way to log. But selective logging may be worse than anyone guessed. The quality of an area may suffer when the best trees are cut down.

This shows slash and burn.

Damage during selective logging is another problem. Selective logging uses equipment that tears up the soil. Thirty trees could be badly hurt by removing just one tree. Logging roads must still be built in the area. These dirt roads damage the forest.

Loggers sometimes build fires to remove brush and wood too small to send to the mill. The fires can burn for days. These fires contribute to air **pollution**.

Loggers build roads to reach trees and to haul logs away. The roads damage the forest. Environmentalists believe logging roads destroy wilderness. There are around 3.5 miles of logging roads for each square mile of land in the Northwest's national forests.

Logging roads cause many problems. Water is one problem. Water evaporates from roads rather than soaking into the ground. During hard rains the road itself changes the way water runs off. This causes floods and clogged streams. The water runoff erodes soil one hundred times faster than normal.

Pollution is another problem with roads in forests. Road dust covers plants, which can kill them. Noise from building roads and from traveling on them scares animals. Logging roads cause there to be fewer animals in the forest.

Some national forest areas are closed to road building because of the problems. But lumber companies have an answer. They sometimes log with helicopters. Helicopters can reach trees and remove logs without roads. Helicopter logging is not without its problems, though. It costs a lot of money.

A helicopter lifts a harvested tree.

Helicopter logging also causes dirtier streams. It dries out the soil. It breaks tree limbs. Many animals leave areas where helicopters are landing.

A forest with no roads into it is called a roadless area. In January 2001, the Roadless Area Conservation Rule was issued by the USDA Forest Service to protect the last remaining forests in our national forest system. But in 2004, the Forest Service logged roadless areas in Oregon after Oregon Governor Ted Kulongoski asked them not to.

President George W. Bush stopped the Roadless Rule in 2005. He left it up to each state to decide. Later that year, California, Oregon, and New Mexico sued President Bush. Washington Governor Christine Gregoire and Oregon Governor Ted Kulongoski asked President Bush to let states return to the Roadless Rule. If not, Governor Gregoire announced Washington would join the three states in their lawsuit.

The Roadless Rule argument is not settled, as of July 2010.

How much of the United States is protected, roadless area?

- Around 2.5 percent (46 million acres) of the United States (not including Hawaii and Alaska) is protected wilderness. If we include Alaska, the number jumps to around 4.5 percent (104 million acres) of protected wilderness.

- Almost two thirds of the national forests have roads. Less than one fifth of the national forests are protected wilderness.

- In the national forests, there are around 380,000 miles of roads.

- National forest roadless areas shrink one to two million acres each year.

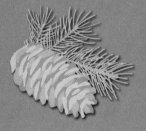

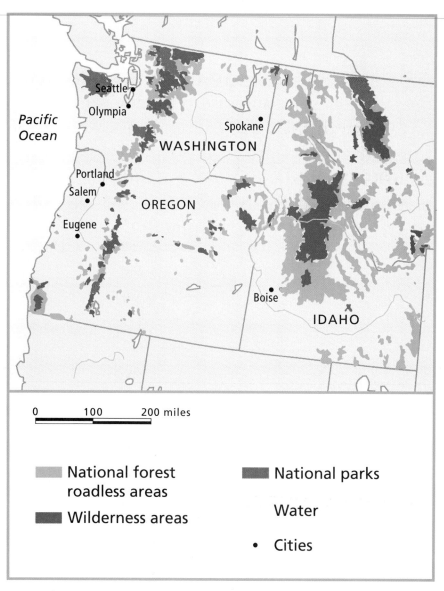

Pacific
Ocean

Seattle
Olympia
Spokane
WASHINGTON

Portland
Salem
OREGON
Eugene

Boise
IDAHO

0   100   200 miles

National forest
roadless areas

Wilderness areas

National parks

Water

• Cities

Map of protected and unprotected areas in the Northwest

CHAPTER 4
Elected Officials Try to Help

Many people are upset over the logging question. It is not surprising that politicians have tried to solve the problem. They have found that there are no easy answers.

In 1993, President William Clinton met with people from all the different groups. He called this meeting a "Forest Summit."

President Clinton tried to save more than 60 million acres of national forests from logging.

A summit is an important meeting. President Clinton hoped to find a **compromise.** He wanted to balance saving the forest with logging the forest.

The Northwest Forest Plan came from this meeting. It was adopted in 1994.

The Northwest Forest Plan protected 70% of the old growth forests. It allowed cutting in the national forests where the spotted owl lived. It protected 7.1 million acres of forest. Less than half of that area was old growth forest. It saved 3.2 million acres for trying out new logging methods. Yet it allowed logging on 4.9 million acres.

Neither side was happy with President Clinton's plan. Lumber businesses wanted more land to log. Environmentalists thought more trees should be protected. Others claimed the spotted owl would not survive. Both sides sued the government. But the court said the Northwest Forest Plan would be followed. For a while, both sides seemed resigned to the way things were.

President Clinton's
Forest Management Plan

- made it possible to harvest and sell timber once again, while still protecting certain forest lands and marshes.

- gave money to the communities in the northwestern United States for training former timber workers in new careers, starting up new businesses in the region, and improving the local water systems.

- labeled certain wetlands and forests as conservation areas to be studied and preserved, and made it possible for individual landowners to help by conserving their own land.

- joined different government agencies together into committees to work on conserving the forest lands and helping the communities.

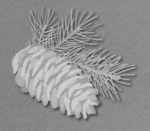

The **federal** government set up land use rules in 1994. The rules protected salmon and **steelhead** from damage caused by logging and other actions along streams. Groups in Washington and Oregon watched over the forest along private rivers.

The Forest Service started a plan to improve the use of land. They wanted to stay away from the problems of endangered animals in the Northwest. But some politicians tried to stop the government from spending money for the plan. President Clinton prevented the politicians from withholding the money.

In 1996, Washington state's Forest Practices Board quit protecting the spotted owl in areas along the Cascades and southwestern Washington. It was now OK to log all the trees in some areas even if there were spotted owl nests.

In 2001, President Clinton increased the Pacific Northwest's federal land. This made more land off limits to logging.

A few months later, a new president was in office. President George W. Bush called an end to President Clinton's efforts.

President Bush increased logging in Northwest federal forests in 2002. He said the purpose of his plan was to prevent forest fires. Environmentalists were against his plan. They said they would sue over increased logging in Washington's spotted owl areas. They waited, though, because they expected the state to fix the problem.

In 2004, President Bush made new rules. His rules gave the Forest Service more say over managing the forests. Environmentalists worried that there would be more careless logging.

CHAPTER 5

Other People Try to Solve the Problem

Politicians work to solve the Northwest logging disagreement. They are not alone. Other people have tried to think of ways to satisfy both sides. Beliefs are not completely wrong or right.

Most environmentalists do not want to give up all wood products. They like having furniture and paper (including toilet paper). Most loggers do not want to log every single tree everywhere. This would get rid of their future jobs. Can the two groups meet in the middle?

One compromise protects old growth but lets young trees to be logged. It's called the "Thinning Plan." This plan would lessen wildfire danger. The plan also calls for the removal of dangerous underbrush and dead trees. These serve as fuel in spreading wildfires.

The plan would leave places for wildlife to live. Trees grow faster in thinned areas. Some people believe thinning might someday return forests to old growth. Thinning should help the forest's health and also give loggers jobs.

Another plan is replanting. Some people believe that planting small trees where trees have been logged is an answer. The area where these forests are located has a dry climate. The old trees pull moisture from deep in the soil. New tiny trees do not have the root systems and so are difficult to grow in dry areas.

This hillside was reforested with numerous small trees surrounded by old forest.

This area was logged after a forest fire.

Logging trees from wildfire areas might seem like another way to solve the problem. The idea is to remove dead trees. Some of the burned trees can be made into lumber to sell. Some people believe this would reduce the risk of more fire. But a recent study led scientists to doubt the plan.

A huge fire named the Biscuit Fire burned in southwestern Oregon in 2002. The fire covered more than 450,000 acres. The area was logged once the fire was out. Later, scientists studied the project. They decided logging slowed down natural regrowth of the forest by 71 percent.

Scientists also pointed out that even the worst forest fire will not kill every tree. The study said that logging increased the chance of another fire. Logging leaves waste that can catch on fire. The scientists decided it was best to let burned forests grow back naturally. This is bad news for timber companies. Logging after fires gives them about 40 percent of the timber they cut from national forests.

Education may hold the key to thoughtful forest care. President Clinton's Northwest Forest Plan asked the Forest Service to provide forest lessons to the community. Some schools provided classes for students. These lessons taught about logging's effects on the **environment**. Some of the students were able to work in the woods with Forest Service workers.

Sometimes environmentalists and loggers sit down together to talk about their ideas. In the small logging town of Quincy, California, a group gathered at the library in 1992. The loggers were out of jobs in the 1980s. They blamed environmentalists. Things got ugly. There were threats and name calling.

Then, the groups decided to work together. They rolled up their shirt sleeves and started talking. The Quincy Library Group met for more than two years. The plan they made allowed for logging of thick undergrowth. It could lessen wildfire danger. It would save the large old trees. It should provide work for loggers. Their plan resulted in the government giving them money. Most of that money goes to forest health projects.

When there are fewer logging jobs, it may be time to get creative about new jobs. Workers in the lumber business can be taught new skills. Some workers are now working for the Forest Service!

In Oregon between 1989 and 1994, 15,000 logging-related jobs were lost. But 20,000 jobs in computer businesses provided new chances for workers. Taking care of tourists also provides other new jobs in Oregon today.

Lumber is still important in Oregon. But people depend less on it for work.

CHAPTER 6

What Can You Do?

You might ask what you can do to help solve the logging problem. Your voice counts. Send elected officials letters and e-mails to tell them what you think. But first, you will want to learn all you can on the subject. You can read books about logging and forests. You can also keep up with the news by reading newspapers and magazines.

There is one more very important way to help the forests: Improve the environment. You can start with your home and school. Use less water. Recycle as much as possible. If every person helped in small ways, it could make a world of difference for our planet.

Glossary

ancient: very old

compromise: an agreement where each side of an argument accepts somewhat less than they really want in order to end the fight

environment: everything that surrounds something including conditions and influences that have to do with its growth

environmentalists: the people who value nature and work to protect it

federal: belonging to the entire nation

harvest: to collect or take, often a crop

lumber: wood sawed into boards

Mayflower: the ship carrying pilgrims to the New World in 1620

mining: digging up minerals

national: belonging to the entire country

oxen: animals related to cows

pastures: lands on which animals graze

pioneers: people who move to unknown areas

pollution: dirty and often dangerous air, water, or soil

private: belonging to one person or group

salamanders: lizard-like animals that live in or near water

salmon: a large fish

selective: carefully chosen

steelhead: a fish that is a type of trout

sued: started a case against someone in a court of law

supported: provided with resources

threatened: endangered

trout: a fish related to salmon

wildlife: wild animals

Index